T0122226

Wailin'
and the
Chicks

Written by
Melanie Wagner

Illustrated by Nicki Forde

Another bee love story

One rainy evening as the cold November winds chased the last sunbeam away, Miss Lily heard a faint cry from the old house next door.

As she crept closer, the sound grew **louder** and **LOUDER** ... until she spotted the tiniest of kittens wailing the **LOUDEST** of noises- peeking out from under the front steps.

3

Now, Miss Lily already had nine cats living in her home, all whom she had rescued from city streets. Brown, orange, and black ones ... striped and spotted ones, and **BIG** ones, and now a new little one, because little Wailin' needed a home.

Carefully tucking that tiny gray kitten into her one hand, Miss Lily headed home, dancing between the raindrops.

Wailin' quickly settled into routine with his new family. He ate ... he played ... he slept ...

And he grew, and **grew**, and **GREW**.

Soon he felt so loved in his new home that he began to play tricks on Miss Lily. One December morning that silly cat climbed the Christmas tree and carefully removed all of the blue glitter ornaments. He hid them under the sofa!

A few years later, his pranks and play seemed less funny to the other cats. They started poking at him trying to chase him away. Soon Wailin' did go away-he hid.

He no longer wanted to play ... even with Miss Lily.

Wise Miss Lily knew this behavior was not normal, so she took Wailin' to see Dr. Amy and Dr. Stephanie at the vet clinic.

Dr. Amy and Dr. Stephanie gently examined Wailin'. They checked his **BIG** eyes, his little ears, and his pink tongue. They even checked his heart. And they drew a blood sample. Miss Lily waited and waited. Soon the doctors appeared with a diagnosis: Wailin' was diabetic. With regular insulin shots and good nutrition, he would be back to pranks and play in no time. Miss Lily was so happy, she whistled a tune all the way home.

Unfortunately, the other cats were not as happy. They were not happy to see Wailin' back home. They also refused to play with him. In fact, they began to pick on him. Poor Wailin'-he felt as if he had lost all of his friends. Even when he promised to stop playing pranks, the others still ignored him.

Now it just so happened that Miss Lily had a friend who had a little farm with chickens. Miss Willa was moving far away and was very sad about leaving her garden. But she was most sad about leaving her chickens.

Hmmmm, thought Miss Lily. **I wonder if the chickens would like to come live in my garden?** As you can imagine, Miss Willa was happy with this plan. Soon she and Miss Lily began planning moving day.

Now, what about Wailin', you ask? **Welllll**, that silly cat put himself in charge of the chickens!

Remembering that playing used to be his favorite pastime, Wailin' thought he would see if these new, funny-looking "cats" wanted to play. He marched himself into Miss Lily's potting shed and invited the chickens to follow. Before Miss Lily and Miss Willa could say, "Cluck, Cluck, Meow," Wailin' and his new friends were marching around the garden!

18

They ate together ... They
took naps together ...

20

But most importantly, they **PLAYED** together. In fact, no other person or animal could get near the chickens without Wailin' wailing. He loved his new friends. And best of all-they loved him. Believe it or not, they loved Wailin' and Miss Lily **SOOOOO** much that those beautiful chickens did not miss their old farm.

Their new family was the best: a cat and eight chickens in a beautiful garden with a potting shed was now home.

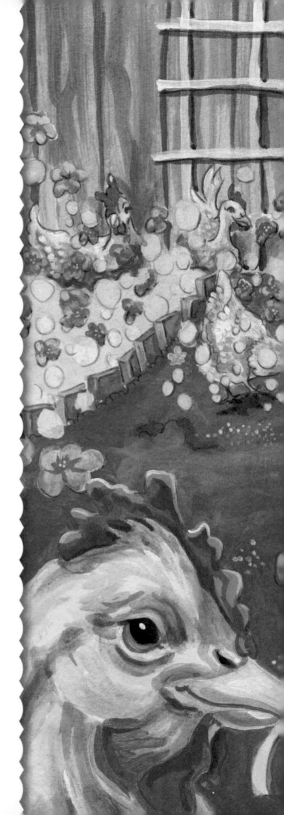

The Beginning

Based on a true story, we are happy to report that Wailin' is now off his blood pressure medicine. And he is managing his diabetes with twice-a-day insulin shots. As for his chicks, they still love to sass him, but they are always happy to share their snacks. Buffy, the oldest chicken, just turned nine.

Copyright © 2021 Melanie Wagner.

All rights reserved. No part of this book may be used or reproduced by any means, graphic, electronic, or mechanical, including photocopying, recording, taping or by any information storage retrieval system without the written permission of the author except in the case of brief quotations embodied in critical articles and reviews.

This book is a work of non-fiction. Unless otherwise noted, the author and the publisher make no explicit guarantees as to the accuracy of the information contained in this book and in some cases, names of people and places have been altered to protect their privacy.

Archway Publishing books may be ordered through booksellers or by contacting:

Archway Publishing
1663 Liberty Drive
Bloomington, IN 47403
www.archwaypublishing.com
844-669-3957

Because of the dynamic nature of the Internet, any web addresses or links contained in this book may have changed since publication and may no longer be valid. The views expressed in this work are solely those of the author and do not necessarily reflect the views of the publisher, and the publisher hereby disclaims any responsibility for them.

Any people depicted in stock imagery provided by Getty Images are models, and such images are being used for illustrative purposes only.
Certain stock imagery © Getty Images.

Interior Image Credit: Nicki Forde

ISBN: 978-1-6657-0174-7 (sc)
ISBN: 978-1-6657-0175-4 (hc)
ISBN: 978-1-6657-0173-0 (e)

Print information available on the last page.

Archway Publishing rev. date: 03/17/2021

Printed in the United States
by Baker & Taylor Publisher Services